Decluttering

A Spirituality of Less

Andrew Barton

Rector of Baughurst and Ramsdell and Wolverton
with Ewhurst and Hannington, Hampshire

GROVE BOOKS LIMITED
RIDLEY HALL RD   CAMBRIDGE   CB3 9HU

Contents

Acknowledgments

My thanks go to Winchester Diocese for the time off for study leave and travel after 15 years with them. Thanks must also go to the Revd Professor Jeremy Begbie at Ridley Hall, Cambridge, the Revds Philip Seddon and Simon Winn for their insights and encouragement, and most especially to the Revds Malcolm and Ruth Lambert in Leicester for their hospitality and cross-cultural experience.

The Cover Illustration is by Peter Ashton

Copyright © Andrew Barton 2006

First Impression May 2006
ISSN 0262-799X
ISBN 1 85174 623 4

Post-Christian Britain?

Ours is an age of the ephemeral and the sound-bite, and first impressions are everything. What philosophies drive this approach to life, and how can Christians begin to counter them today?

We live in an age of plenty. Ideas, relationships and goods amass—but do not last. By contrast, the promises of God are eternal and the good news is unchanging. Jesus Christ is the same yesterday, today and forever, but institutions like the church are seen as clubs for the initiated and the like-minded, not for everyone. Faith is just one more lifestyle to take or leave as one thinks fit.

The 2001 census revealed that a majority of people still wish to describe themselves as 'Christian' (71%—or some 42 million). Yet the country is far from Christian despite a lingering belief in a god of some sort.[1] Depressingly, 43% of people in Britain in a recent poll could not say what Easter celebrated,[2] and only 33% of the British public in another survey considered that religion was important.[3]

So just how do Christians make an impact in a country that is forgetting its religious heritage? How do we respond to a fast-paced, shallow society that sees the church as old and tired? Do we shrug our shoulders and despair, unable to fathom how to reach out to a lost society? Do we sit back and wait for God to bring the predestined 'saved' into our churches? (I think that is what many of us do in fact do!) Or maybe we wait for Walt Disney to bring out the next movie in the *Narnia* series in order to take along non-Christian friends?

Alternatively, we might 'go with the flow' and try to offer cutting-edge ideas. The most recent approaches by church organizations have been to look for points of contact with society. These have mostly involved dialogue with other philosophies and theologies, such as in talking to those with New Age beliefs,[4] as well as offering a less structured way of 'doing church' that speaks to our radically individualistic culture.[5]

These approaches form part of the traditional means of evangelism that we find Jesus and the apostles adopting as they move from Jerusalem and Judea and Samaria to the ends of the earth (Acts 1.8, 17.22ff). But that movement was into a pre-Christian culture by definition. The challenge today is how to witness in a post-Christendom society—one that has laws and behavioural norms that only have a nominal and vestigial Christian underpinning.

Inevitably, any evangelistic success in reaching out to a person or group will eventually involve them joining a fellowship of faith, whether it meet in a home or a church building. However, most people are suspicious of the church. As Russ Hughes of St Luke's, Maidstone aptly put it, 'The church has done for Jesus what *Jaws* did for swimming lessons.'[6] That is not to say that society is particularly anti-Christian; there are only a few antagonistic commentators like Richard Dawkins[7] or Polly Toynbee.[8] Christians are rarely caricatured as intolerant fundamentalists on a clandestine mission to a secular country. Nevertheless, the gospel message is a radical dislocation from the values of a selfish and insecure world, so its promotion must be in ways that are comprehensible to those who do not yet realize that there is Good News to be found.

As the body of Christ, we need to communicate the deep truths of God. If that proclamation is to a world where the average attention span is measured in minutes or seconds, then other approaches of a more visual nature are needed than just someone preaching on a street corner. We know that the gospel message makes a real difference, but if we give the impression of being little different from everyone else, just how do we convey this radically distinctive message? We need to be a visible sign of gospel values in all aspects of life, not just in beliefs and values. Without this, society will just look at the outward things and find us wanting.

The objective of this book is to promote decluttering to achieve this. Decluttering is about divesting ourselves of scattered or disordered things that reduce how effectively we live our lives. Such things may be ideas, events, or physical possessions. Decluttering is about living with less, and about creating spiritual wellbeing. In 15 years of ministry I have been invited into many Christian, and non-Christian, homes but have rarely found anything that looked outwardly distinctive between the two categories. Indeed, in many Christian homes, Jesus' appeal about not storing up treasure on earth often appears to have been omitted from the family Bible. In contrast, a few homes of non-Christians have appeared more peaceful and restful and conveyed a greater sense of calm, even though their hearts were not in heaven.

Three Influences

Before we look at what value decluttering may have, it is worth reflecting on the major influences in today's society. For unless we recognize what drives the lives of many people today we may miss the mark in assessing how we show others an extra spiritual dimension of life that is based on the joy and peace that Christ gives.

There appear to be three ways of thinking, or philosophies, of which we should take note. They are not mutually exclusive, but they do form a helpful set of influences that need to be addressed if we are to proclaim the gospel more effectively.

Postmodern Thinking

Postmodernism describes not a single belief but a movement that is found as an influence in art, literature, philosophy and architecture. It refers to the end of modernity (characterized by ideas of progress and absolutes) and its replacement by more local, personalized worldviews. Jean-François Lyotard, the French socialist philosopher, famously defined postmodernity as 'incredulity toward meta-narratives,' meaning that in the era of postmodern culture, people have rejected the grand, supposedly universal stories provided by religion, capitalism, history and gender that have defined society and conduct in the past, and instead have begun to organize their cultural life around a variety of individualistic beliefs.[9]

This aversion to the generalities or grand narratives of a larger group is symptomatic of today's postmodern thinking. Overwhelmed by countless new communication possibilities, the instinctive individual response is to retreat into a privatized world with its personalized beliefs and value systems.[10] Colin Horseman writes how as a clergyman he struggled to get any fifth form (year 12) students to find any abiding principles to govern personal relationships.[11] Their response was fiercely individualistic — truth is not an absolute. My truth is not necessarily your truth!

In such circumstances appeal to the Bible or any ecclesiastical authority is unlikely to be successful. What is needed is that we become the aroma of Christ, a fragrance from life to life (2 Corinthians 2.15, 16). In a society that believes everything is relative and there are no right paths to follow, it is our lives and lifestyle that need to go under the spotlight to show that this idea is false.

Consumerism

The power of consumerism is all too apparent today. The popular mantra, corrupting Descartes, is 'I shop, therefore I am.' Consumerism is based on programming. We are taught to buy what someone wants to sell us. It upholds a marketplace view of the world. It is consumption for capitalism's sake, feeding on individualistic hedonism and escapism in the form of 'retail therapy.'

But although aimed at consumers as individuals, the self is largely forgotten in this process. Richard Rorty has suggested that where there is no centre to the self in a consumer society we are almost rudderless, and our actions and indeed we ourselves are mere historical contingencies.[12] Our sole response to the world, which is characterized as a large marketplace, is little other than to become aware of the distinction between force and persuasion. What we want or what we need defines us.

Without any core set of guiding beliefs, the only goal is what Cardinal Cormac Murphy O'Connor has termed 'transient happiness.'[13] For retailers and manufacturers the competition then is to capture the hearts and minds of consumers. The means is everything and lasting, the ends are nothing and disposable. Consumerism needs to have at its heart an immediate and inbuilt obsolescence. Indeed, the thrill of buying is paramount in consumerism. It gives in to greed, and the notion that 'more is beautiful.'

Such an attitude is completely contrary to the gospel. God's care for us as individuals is real and lasting, an inheritance that will not rust or fade (1 Peter 1.4). Although the Old Testament indicates that material wealth is a gift from God, slavery to it is a curse. Within consumerist society Christians can exercise other priorities apart from selfishness in buying. One example is in the purchase of Fairtrade products, now offered in many shops, that give a slightly greater return to Third-World producers, and that begins to reverse the history of exploitation.[14] Julie Kelly points out that as Christians we should be discerning over consumer choices. If we want a secular world to listen, actions are needed that speak louder than words.[15] Again it is our whole lifestyle, our spirituality in practice, which will be on display.

Liquid Living

Life itself is increasingly 'liquid,' according to the sociologist Zygmunt Bauman.[16] This is an age where nothing can be taken for granted. The idea of 'a job for life' has gone in society, and seems about to disappear in Christian ordained ministry. The solid pillars of life, expressed in traditional mantras such as 'a good education will always get you work,' have dissolved. Life is indeterminate, often capricious and erratic, and the quickening pace of life leads to less time for anything.

Bauman notes that 'liquid life' is a precarious life; a succession of new beginnings as new challenges come along.[17] Survival in society is consequently based on how quickly we can adapt to new technology, situations and events. Think of the speed at which the Internet has become part of our lives in the form of on-line ordering, or communication via email. We need to run to keep up with a changing world of new consumer opportunities where endings are almost more important than beginnings. Discarding, detoxing, de-skilling are simply processes in the ongoing task of life-long change that enable people to adapt to an ever-changing work and lifestyle environment, rather than help them to lead a more balanced or spiritual existence.

Such a view of life is frightening. As with consumerism, only a few are successful and most are not. The best most of us can do is to try to keep up with the pace of change according to this view. It is in complete contrast to the value of each person created in God's image, which inherently makes them loved, and defines that they should be valued by others around them.

Response

How can Christians engage with a world where change, consumption, and precariousness characterize life? Steve Hollinghurst notes that 'It is not enough for us to speak of another way; we must live this out. Indeed it is not enough for us to speak of the transforming power of Christ unless it can be seen in us.'[18] Paul in his letter to his beloved Philippian congregation says (Phil 4.9), 'Keep on doing the things that you have learned and received and heard and seen in me, and the God of peace will be with you.' Peter too emphasizes this in his first letter, often thought to be a tract to the newly baptized (1 Peter 2.9), 'Beloved, I urge you as aliens and exiles to abstain from the desires of the flesh that wage war against the soul.'

Decluttering, I would like to suggest, is a process of contemporary life that can be employed in order that our relationship with God be more apparent to those around. It is about possessions and the way we accumulate them. Consumerism, change and individualism give us no limits to this acquisitiveness. Our appetites are titivated so that an addiction is created for more. It is not just drugs that do this! We hide such cravings with phrases such as 'an increase in the standard of living,' or 'we are better off than our parents.' Christians will want to look elsewhere for seeking what satisfies (John 4.14), and it will be noticed. However, Jesus does warn us about looking pious in prayer and fasting (Matt 6.5–8), but in this ever more visual age the Christian whose life is really challenging in appearance is going to attract comment and enquiry. This is about spiritual living and it needs to proclaim what is of primary importance to us.

Jesus himself in the Sermon on the Mount emphasizes this in his teaching on prosperity (Matt 6.19–21), 'Do not store up for yourselves treasures on earth, where moth and rust consume and where thieves break in and steal; but store up for yourselves treasures in heaven, where neither moth nor rust consumes and where thieves do not break in and steal. For where your treasure is, there your heart will be also.' It is not about looking different just to be noticed. It is about proclaiming what is of foundational importance in our lives. In the next chapter we will look at how God's people have responded to this call in the past. It led these early Christian communities to attempt to live with less to be true to the gospel call; can we heed their example?

2

Does the Bible give us any examples of how living with less might bring us closer to God?

Recently, I visited the Sinai Peninsula. I had been unaware just how desolate the area was, especially around Mount Sinai, but the wilderness described in Exodus 19 is utterly barren. Yet this was where Moses and indeed the people of Israel met God face to face (Deut 5.1), and where Israel received God's word when there were no other distractions (except those like the golden calf that they made themselves!).

Later, the prophets (see, for example, Jer 2.6, Hosea 11.1, Amos 2.10) looked back wistfully to this time when the God of their fathers led them out of slavery, directing them with pillars of cloud and fire (Exod 13.21), detailing the making of a portable tent temple (Exod 25ff), and leading them on to the Promised Land. They became God's first pilgrim people. Uncluttered as nomads, they relied totally on God for physical food (manna, quails) and spiritual sustenance, but they also became more organized. Laws of purity, behaviour, and provisions for sacrifice were given, as well as forming an army to meet inevitable unfriendly kings and unwelcoming cities. Instead of the first-born belonging to the Lord, the tribe of Levi performed this function of priesthood (Num 3.11–13). They were even organized in their movement according to tribes in great detail (Num 2–5). Organization and order formed the backdrop to this mobile worshipping community who were following God's leading, and living obediently in the desert.

Organization and order formed the backdrop to this mobile worshipping community who were following God's leading

Old Testament scholars rightly emphasize a dislocation between the Mosaic era and the Royal period. In the former period God directed Israel through Moses and Aaron and then Joshua. However, when God's chosen people entered the Promised Land they were given instructions about not becoming like nations around them with permanent temples (1 Sam 7.5–7) and kings (1 Sam 8.7ff). God permitted these things but with ominous warnings. 1 Samuel 8 lists the dangers of slavishly following surrounding cultures, and even when King

Solomon began to construct the Temple at Jerusalem there is reference to the forced labour needed from the people of Israel (1 Kings 5.13). The parallels with Egypt were clear, and God only reluctantly grants this arrangement.[19]

It seems that God would prefer that we travel light through life. He knows that power and wealth can be effective antidotes to a spiritual life (Deut 8.17f). Riches and cultural syncretism came as inevitable temptations and spiritual distractions to the kings and people of Israel, even wise Solomon (1 Kings 11.4). It led to exile, scattering of the tribes and a lesser nation as a result.

Equally, in New Testament times, Jesus' encounter with the rich man who had many possessions gives an identical message (Mark 10.17–22) to the dire warnings of Deuteronomy. There is a radical basis to the Good News that will mean that the world, with all its excesses, will inevitably hate his followers (John 15.19).

To find permanent rest Christians have to look beyond the physical world

Jesus warned his disciples that they would be driven out of synagogues (John 16.2), and Paul tells us how they would meet in homes (for example Rom 16.5, Col 4.15). Yet, in 30 years or so, these few people had turned the world upside down (Acts 17.6). These new pilgrim people had no lasting city in this world, like their Master (Heb 12.13f), but a legacy of the Promised Land that goes beyond this world, to one which will last and 'cannot be shaken' (Heb 12.28). To find permanent rest Christians have to look beyond the physical world.[20] Indeed, in Revelation, sin is not merely disobedience against God, but blind involvement in material concerns, just as the world practises in its excesses of greed, avarice and exploitation (Rev 2.14f, 17.1f).

If these believers made a difference two millennia ago, how might we, given the new fast-paced world we live in? We have life so much easier. Civic authorities tolerate us, there is no Caesar to worship in any sanctioned state cult, and our leaders do not aspire to divinity (yet!). Indeed, with so many negatives to combat in their societies, how did the early church make such headway?

Michael Green notes that the early church was characterized by a lack of altars, temples and priesthood. They were unified, local, and mobile; for example Aquila and Priscilla are found ministering at Corinth, Ephesus and Rome (Acts 18.2, 18.24, Rom 16.3). Green writes, 'We have a far higher capability for mobility than they had, yet how stuck in ruts many Christians are. We are not willing to move house and go somewhere else if the Lord calls us. We are burdened with possessions, which we deem all but indispensable…I guess we need to sit a good deal less tight to possessions, houses, to educational facilities, to all the things which conspire to peg us down in one place…these revolutionaries certainly were not.'[21]

Present too in the New Testament community was a great sense of hospitality. Their homes were open to any who might come preaching and evangelizing. A deep quality of love, friendship, and an attractive lifestyle not based on excess, waste or selfishness will be part of what will be noticed by a suspicious generation, just as it was then.

Although we should not be so simplistic as to expect an exact parallel with our church life today, there is a sense in which we need to be aware just how valuable the experience of the New Testament church can be to our situation. There was order to some extent, but not rigidity. For example, in their evangelistic zeal they did not create an exact set of orders of ministry. Colin Buchanan notes how the titles bishop (*episkopos*) and presbyter (*presbuteros*) are used interchangeably, and deacon (*diakonos*) can be translated as a minister or servant.[22]

Such flexibility was lost to some extent after the New Testament period by the need to organize a rapidly growing church. This growth caused a move out of homes such as those mentioned in the New Testament into larger buildings that became 'holy spaces' for meeting God. This movement reached its climax with the building of the great cathedrals across the world. Mighty impressive structures as they are, the consequence was that the ordinary home became less of a significant setting for worship and gathering of God's people.

These people did not follow an ascetic life because they thought it was fashionable to do so

Equally, the earliest Christian monks, known as the 'Desert Fathers,' inhabited the deserts of the Middle East, such as in Egypt, from the third century AD onwards. They left a legacy of sayings and traditions, mostly from meditating on Scripture. These are the foundation upon which later monastic leaders, including St Benedict, built their rules of life. Down the centuries they sought places of solitude and self-discipline that gave space for them to practise the presence of God, and to seek after holiness and wisdom as individual hermits. They rejected excess, luxury, avarice and possessions. Their motivation was in wishing to obey Scriptures of self-denial (for example Matt 19.21). These people did not follow an ascetic life because they thought it was fashionable to do so, but because they considered they were being true to biblical commands. They were not running from the world but were rather seeking to turn to Christ and allowing him to transform them completely.[23] Later, as monastic life developed from a developing community life, young men were still attracted away from home life by the writings of these saints.

Worship centre and home were two different places. In Britain, even before the Industrial Revolution began, housing reflected an existence that centred on eating and sleeping and raising a family. Work was conducted increasingly away from the home, with activities concerning the life of the Christian community focussed in parish church buildings, which then acted as centres of social life.

After the emergence of Reformation churches, which brought about translation of Latin services and the Bible into the common language, change emerged through the ministry of preachers like John Wesley who were driven out of mainstream denominations. Such Christians were forced by necessity to meet again in home settings. In the 20th century the rise in the number of house churches showed just how much the church needed to return to homes to offset the over-rigid and often impersonal character that it had acquired in the public's mind. Small was beautiful once again, and without expensive church buildings to keep up, this freed resources to enable them to concentrate on spiritual and numerical growth. Wolfgang Simson writes how house churches are meant to function like 'a spiritual extended family, relational, spontaneous and organic.'[24] It was a return to the church's biblical roots.

If spiritual life returns into the home setting, and non-Christians continue to imagine the local church to be merely a cold, uninviting building, how should our homes be transformed in order that we are seen as a group of people whose life and values show something of the joy of the Good News of Jesus Christ? In the next chapter we will look at three examples of decluttering to set the scene for the practical process that is being proposed.

3

Life today is fast-paced, stressed and materialistic. We need to declutter our hearts, our workloads, and our homes to counter the effects.

Life today has become so full of activity and effort of all kinds that we are at overload, as well as suffering from infostress and infofatigue (two recent web-words!). According to Australian newspaper *The Age* people are finding it harder and harder to process all that comes at them.[25] We have to prioritize activities to an extent no generation has before. Prioritizing means a selection, and that in turn needs to be based on a set of underlying principles. But we need not only to prioritize, but also to cease doing what is neither beneficial nor useful. As content management expert Gerry McGovern noted in the same article in *The Age*, 'Working harder will only make the problem worse.'

Instead of working harder, can we work smarter, with better priorities and clearer goals?

Prioritizing means a selection, and that in turn needs to be based on a set of underlying principles

Decluttering is about resisting being overwhelmed, be it by information, choices, or physical things. David Ford notes that we have three resources to combat the feeling of having our lives overwhelmed.[26] Firstly we must acknowledge this, and secondly name the pressures we are under. Naming things has a powerful effect through bringing them into language. Then there is a need to describe these feelings in order to achieve the third response of coping. Below are three examples of decluttering responses that seek to achieve this.

Decluttering Hearts and Lives—Lenten Practice

In the Christian year, the season of Lent, which means 'holy spring,' is a particular time when spiritual spring-cleaning is addressed. Each year the 40 days provide a weekly venue for published courses to work through how we may best let God 'create and make in us new and contrite hearts,' as the 1662 *Book of Common Prayer* collect for Ash Wednesday says. This involves the call of both John the Baptist and Jesus to repent and believe (Mark 1.4 and 1.15), to turn from old ways to a new one based on faith in the kingdom of God in their midst. We declutter by naming and turning away from certain habits to embrace the joy of gospel life.

In their Lent courses for 2005 and 2006, Robert Warren and Sue Mayfield look at how the Sabbath can become a springboard for finding a more ordered and peaceful approach to life. They write in their introduction to *Life Balance*, 'Sabbath is an attitude not just a day. Sabbath invites us to take its principles of resting, thanksgiving, justice and generosity into the whole of life — reducing the stress and rush and enlarging our vision.' The structure of their course rightly focuses on a much needed rest from a hectic world and allows time to Pause, Celebrate, Rest, Play, and Liberate.[27] This is a process that needs to be cultivated not just through Lent but for the rest of the year too. Without an active resolution to keep our own life decluttered, any benefit can soon evaporate.

Perhaps the best-known post-biblical example of decluttering is to be found in the writings of St Augustine. In his *Confessions* in Books I-VII he spells out in detail examples of his many wilful errors of thought and belief, and morals in relationships (be it with his lover(s), mother or son). He bitterly regrets his hedonistic lifestyle, which ultimately gave him no more than fleeting happiness before he became a Christian.

The entire *Confessions* is an extended prayer to God, providing an autobiography of this sinner being turned into a saint, a process that ends in a conversion experience at the close of Book VIII. The effect is to make him desire to go in a new direction, forgiven and freed from past sins. In Book IX he writes, 'But it was in my inmost heart, where I had grown angry with myself, where I had been stung with remorse, where I had slain my old self and offered it in sacrifice, where I had first purposed to renew my life and had placed my hope in you and had made me glad at heart.'

The summary of his conversion is contained in his famous phrase (in Book I), 'you made us for yourself, and our hearts find no peace, until they rest in you.'[28] Augustine's *Confessions* provide a vulnerable, self-giving openness of how saints are not born, just recreated from sinners. *Confessions* is a classic because of Augustine's ruthless assessment and naming of his own failings in ideas, beliefs and morality, together with a very frank assessment of his feelings in the face of finding a God who loves him. He declutters what is wrong in his life as a model repentant sinner.

Decluttering Events—Church Service Overload

In 2005 Christmas Day fell on a Sunday. Inevitable protests came when some US mega-churches decided to close, and not hold services on the day when the church celebrates Christ's birth.[29] Willow Creek Church near Chicago shut its doors (albeit after large services in the week before Christmas). The Revd Gene Appel, senior pastor of Willow Creek, is quoted as saying, 'We do not see it as not having church on Christmas. We see it as decentralizing the church on Christmas—hundreds of thousands of experiences going on around Christmas trees. The best way to honour the birth of Jesus is for families to have a more personal experience on that day.'[30]

Whether or not these churches were right to do this is not my point. In the case of Willow Creek, the leaders faced the fact that family togetherness came top at the end of a busy week of worship. Their lives were becoming cluttered with services and worship itself was detracting from a balanced life as the body of Christ.

In my own rural benefice I know that only a few families run each church. The pressures at weekends mean that many Sunday services are not always well attended. Commuting and long working hours mean that what once fitted into a week now has to be fitted into a weekend. Other pressures are shopping on Sundays; dispersed families needing visiting; cheap (yet much-needed) weekend breaks; non-Christian children's activities; and even personal time. All these and more constrain both Christians and non-Christians into a cultural straightjacket that is becoming increasingly accepted because it seems an inescapable part of everyday life. What seems to combat this in my benefice is to have special services promoted more—rogation services, services with guest speakers, as well as highlighting the important festivals. In this way everything is not of equal priority, and this means that more effort may be put in (and equally a more positive response brought about), whilst some services simply do not happen!

We needed to declutter our service structure because we had neither the resources, nor the money, nor the staffing to keep up a historical rota built up when lay peoples' lives were more parish-based. Because church members were less likely to be given a role to fulfil for years, volunteers became more numerous.

Decluttering for Selling—The House Doctor

TV makeover programmes, and those about selling surplus possessions, abound. They usually have an end of financing other ventures. It is particularly noticeable that in programmes such as *House Doctor*, decluttering is a necessary first stage. This is decluttering with the purpose of selling a house that has been on the market for a long period. It begins with the sellers recognizing something that needs addressing, and an emotional naming of what it might entail to achieve it. Then follows an attempt to strip the property of individual character to make the property more saleable. This involves decluttering by removing a large proportion of the personal effects of the owner. Usually this is achieved with some reluctance on the part of the sellers, but often a financial pragmatism takes over, and they cope. The result should be that potential buyers of the property are able to see themselves moving in with the minimum of changes being immediately necessary—because a buyer is equally overloaded by busyness and is as worried about price as the seller! But that is not before we hear how they (and equally we as viewers) are wedded to material possessions and the clutter they accumulate. After decluttering, selective redecoration and more impersonal but fresher re-dressing of many of the rooms takes place, as well as a clearer identification and demarcation of the uses of each room.

What happens after this is that the makeover suddenly begins to entice the current owners. The house becomes a place of calm and simplicity that is attractive to people in our frantic culture. What may have attracted the owners about the house in the first place becomes evident once again. There is a liberating experience in many cases where the makeover is well done. Less is more as rooms are emptied of non-essential furniture, and colour balances and space make rooms more welcoming. Rooms often revert to an original purpose; for example, a junk room is turned back into the bedroom it was designed to be, before it got filled up. Prospective buyers can then picture themselves living in the house more readily. Decluttering has done its job.

One young couple I married recently had just moved into a new house and had completely divested themselves of possessions in the process and bought new ones. The overall result was the creation of a peaceful and tranquil home, and it is a real joy to visit.

Decluttering can be a powerful process in changing the lives of those who undergo it

These brief examples of decluttering illustrate that this can be a powerful process in changing the lives of those who undergo it. Our mission is to influence and witness to others of the Good News, and our Christian faith provides us with principles and values for building new lives transformed by God's power.

In the next chapter we will outline ways and means of physical decluttering to create homes that aid us in promoting our faith. We will look at an example of how a particular type of design might help us to declutter and to produce a home that is attractive and might reflect something of our Christian faith, and also explore how in multi-cultural Britain there is an example from other faith groups that may help us.

4 Practical Decluttering

Reasons for Decluttering

There are, of course, many reasons why people, Christians and non-Christians alike, might seek to declutter their homes. Life changes happen inevitably in today's liquid world. Family changes can occur though bereavement, marriage and family break-up, or children leaving home. The pressures of work can mean that we seek a much greater sanctuary in our homes; or maybe the inevitability of moving home in order to start a new job forces us to assess essentials rather than move with all the goods we have accumulated.

For Christians, if we are disciplined in this physical aspect of our lives, it will reinforce an approach that seeks to discipline other behavioural aspects of our lives. It will highlight to others our character, tastes, wealth, fears and aspirations more clearly than anything we might say about ourselves.[31] If we verbally witness to a simple gospel of grace, and yet our lives and our homes witness the reverse, it should be no surprise if we are ineffective evangelists because we are sending out mixed messages.

Whatever the reasons for this process being undertaken, what influences might be of help to us as we declutter? Here are two.

Minimalism

Minimalism describes a particular way of approaching art and design, concentrating on functionality, form and simplicity. It is about emphasizing the fundamentals of a number of areas, about design not only in architecture, but also in the performing arts (such as in the music of Philip Glass, or the plays of Samuel Beckett). Minimalist poetry, such as Japanese Haiku, is about incisive observation with few descriptive words. *Wikipedia*, the Internet encyclopaedia, notes how minimalism is often 'applied to groups or individuals practicing asceticism and the reduction of physical possessions and needs to a minimum.'[32]

Minimalism in architecture was influential following the work of the British designer John Pawson in his book *Minimum*. Although he promoted a Zen Buddhist approach that rejected possessions and looked to simplicity as a path to self-enlightenment, the essence of wishing to promote a decluttered lifestyle is not dependent on one particular (non-Christian) religion. Simone Schleifer notes in her editorial in *Minimalist Interiors*, 'In our materialistic society, dominated by technology and revolving around information, the most important decision involves deciphering what is truly essential to life and being able to embrace modernity with only a few carefully selected possessions.'[33]

Such minimalist ideas are those that a Christian can legitimately look at and usefully mine. This is not to accept uncritically any philosophies or theologies that often come with such movements (such as *feng sui*), but to explore how our homes may reflect something of the peace and the priorities in life that following Christ gives. In the case of cathedrals, the peace that is afforded by the emphasis on space and solitude is conducive to contemplative spirituality. In a busy and frantic world tranquillity becomes a valuable commodity.

A minimalist approach does not mean that we neglect convenience. Indeed, many minimalist buildings are models of space-saving and elegant and useful designs.[34] They are just not over-elaborate. Minimalist interiors, whether homes or hotels, are generally characterized by being bright, often white, with subtle use of lighting and promotion of space. They promote peaceful surroundings that are easy to live in, whilst being functional. They often give an impression of being oases of calm—dark colours are frequently mixed with light colours to give contrast, but never attempt to jar on the eye. They are often a far cry from the furniture laden, multi-use rooms that characterize British homes.

British Asian Homes

We need not be slaves to a largely secular history of home interiors based on mid 18th/19th century industrialization with front parlour, living/back room and kitchen. Most of us will never be able to afford the luxury of a custom designed minimalist home, but that does not mean that we cannot personalize our house interiors. Indeed for those who come from overseas to live in Britain, this is exactly what they have done.

For example, the parishes in the north of the city centre of Leicester have more than a distinctive multi-cultural feel. Some 60% are Hindu, 15% are Sikh, 5% Muslim. Anglican Church attendance in Leicestershire has fallen from 2% to 1% in the past 15 years and the number of stipendiary clergy from 200 to 130 in the diocese. Christians here are distinctly a minority culture in this multi-ethnic area. Whilst historically buoyant denominations like Methodists have all but disappeared, all main Christian denominations in fact struggle.

With such a high ethnic minority mix there are significant areas where the differing lifestyles are apparent. Victorian and later-date detached and semi-detached housing is often significantly modified inside and out to reflect the larger 'extended family' situations as well as religious lifestyle. In fact, the house is seen as plastic to their religious and cultural needs. The outside of the house may often be greatly modified to show the wealth and concomitant social and caste status (as reflected in the area, too, which in turn reflects house prices). Front gardens are often concreted over to provide parking space for a car (size often again reflecting status), and elaborate PVC window units, side extensions and even Greek-style columns! This also happens to the rear of the property, reducing garden size to almost zero. Gardens are a particular pastime of those with leisure time and a cultural history of gardening.

Ground floor furniture follows a minimalist line but mostly for religious reasons. A devout Hindu family will worship on the ground floor, and so space is needed. The spaces are therefore redefined over the traditional sitting room and living/dining room layout. Here then it is for a different reason that clutter is not needed or wanted. Infrastructure is modified to meet specific needs of the cultural and religious constraints placed upon people by their history and tradition.

In the 1980s, it was a Christian vogue for special parts of a house to be set aside as a quiet place for someone to reflect and pray. Many Christian homes still have these *poustinias*. *Poustinia* is a Russian word to describe a simple wooden hut that is just big enough to shelter a single person making a prayer-ful retreat for several days in the silence of the forest. It says something of our lack of distinctiveness in modern society that we are not trying to make *all* of our homes places of peace (rather than one special room) and therefore places where our faith is seen as vitally important by those who come to visit, whatever rooms they go into. This should be true whether we have a house church, or a cell church, or no church meetings in our homes.

Ten Steps to Practical Decluttering

In 2005, after eleven years in my current post, my rectory was hopelessly cluttered. Like many people, I do not consider myself a hoarder in any obsessive way, yet things naturally accumulate if one lives a busy life. However, increasingly, car keys and mobile phones went missing for days and the time taken to search for them was increasing. Additionally, cleaning meant moving items that were parked in odd places, and in order to sit down, items frequently had to be moved to such places. It was only when a new parishioner looked shocked at the state of my study that I decided that I had to 'do a declutter'!

It soon became more of a spiritual exercise to recover a peace that has been overlaid with the things of this world

What I learnt about this process of decluttering was that it soon became more of a spiritual exercise to recover a peace that has been overlaid with the things of this world. It was about less, in order to achieve more. The decluttering process, room by room, was largely as follows:

1 Admit Your Cluttering Weakness
Whereas children are often scolded for leaving toys around, adults leave personal items such as old magazines, books and sundry personal items. Repentance is not only for children!

2 Realize That This is a Lengthy Process, But Persist
Clutter inexorably builds up, so the process of decluttering is equally going to be lengthy and take time and effort. I scheduled two months for my large rectory.

3 Begin by Creating Storage Space
In my case, storage space and furniture were filled up with books and clothes, and old computers. I needed to assess what was actually needed. Some furniture was simply there to provide storage for old items that had not been discarded! Books and clothes were disposed of to charity shops where appropriate, and theology books to needy ordinands. Do not readily fill the storage space as you declutter other rooms.

4 Allocate Regular Time to Declutter
A regular hour a day, perhaps two on weekend days, is likely to yield results, whereas an irregular effort will reap few rewards. This is a big task, and to achieve a result little and often is best. It is easy to become compulsive about decluttering, and burn yourself out quickly. Be dedicated, attack the problem head on, certainly, but control your passion.

5 Buy Aids to Decluttering
Heavy-duty black sacks are a must in decluttering, and it is likely that a paper shredder is too. Decades of back bank statements may need your attention.

6 Do Not Delegate Your Decluttering
Admit at the start that your family are unlikely to comply with your newfound enthusiasm. They require gently cajoling and watching over. Decluttering requires dedication and constant supervision.

7 Be Adventurous with What You Discard
Local companies may well exist that will find a home for that television or piece of furniture surplus to requirements. You will be surprised what can be found a good home.

8 Be Systematic in Each Room

It is best to work around each room methodically. Do not leave areas considered too difficult or you will be likely to be happy to live with it again. Remove items that belong elsewhere but be cautious of moving them to decluttered rooms, unless you have already allocated a place for them.

9 Be Ruthless

If an item of whatever size has remained in a place unused since you moved in, do you really need it? Sell it (try *eBay* or equivalent), store it (the Americans are 'into' self-storage in a big way) or dispose of it (obviously in an ecologically responsible way). This is the most difficult step to get through, for we seem 'made for excess,' as David Ford puts it.[35] We love our possessions, and they possess us.

10 Reassess Room Functions

Consider what you are actually using rooms for and consider changing the function of any spare rooms (for example, turn it into a quiet room, or a guest room—and then pray to get some guests!). Rooms that have multiple uses are unlikely to be areas of tranquillity.

The whole decluttering process can permeate into other areas of our life if we let it

The whole decluttering process, suitably prayed over, can be a cathartic exercise and the amazing thing is that it can permeate into other areas of our life if we let it. In busy lives we can give ourselves permission to live with fewer plans, have decreased but more realistic goals and expectations, and enjoy an agenda that is more realistically achievable—all in order that we may give ourselves over to recognizing the presence of God in our lives.

There are also certain spin-off benefits to this process. One is that living with less is likely to result in a greater disposable income. Using this for hospitality or providing for the needs of the poor are two suggestions for dealing with this. Equally, as Nick Helm notes, the spaces created in our homes are 'safe spaces'—there is freedom from external interruption if we are careful, freedom from internal interruption and the agendas of others that need dealing with, and a more secure boundary to acceptance and confidentiality for visitors and residents as compared with a church building.[36]

Like all practical spiritualities this is a not a single procedure to be done when a crisis is reached. God prefers not to work that way with us. Just as we must practise the presence of God in our lives to develop a life of prayer, daily worship and witness, it is in the practice of constant decluttering that new space and freedoms will be discovered.

Living with Less

5

Decluttering is inherently a process of loss, and some may struggle with it. But it can lead to new beginnings and witnesses to the hope in us.

In reading about this process of decluttering, you may have felt that your home, or those of people you know, does not need decluttering. Some objections may be voiced as follows.

Is this Imposing Law, Rather than the Gospel of Grace?

No. But the early Christians were reminded by Paul not to use grace as a reason for trampling on the Law (Rom 6.1), and Timothy was similarly instructed to ensure his lifestyle accorded with the gospel (1 Tim 4.11–16). Should we do less in any aspects of modern life? Law should not be an end in itself because we all fall short (Rom 3.23) but neither should it be seen as irrelevant to the outworking of salvation (Phil 2.12). Living with less is a means of grace as with all spiritual disciplines; it is a joy, not servitude. Whilst we live as servants of God, the Son has set us free indeed (John 8.36).

Do I Have to Look Odd Simply to be Noticed as a Christian?

Again no. But in this age of individualism there is a great pressure to be conformers to the spirit of the age. In Monty Python's irreverent *Life of Brian,* the main character exhorts the crowd not to see him as a messiah but to think for themselves—'You are all individuals,' he proclaims. 'We are all individuals,' they slavishly reply! The Christian faith is a radical dissent from a world of luxury that has been a constant snare enticing people to participate in an excess that destroys.

Decluttering Seems to Imply an Outcome that Looks Austere—Surely Christian Homes Should be Cosy and Welcoming?

This is a valid point, but my main aim in suggesting it as a process is as a response to the rampant culture of materialism that invades all our lives. Christian homes should always be friendly and inviting, just as our characters should be, but we need to assess exactly what all aspects of our lives communicate. Decluttering is an outward physical example of the spiritual peace that must be part of our lives. It is 'sacramental' in the sense of reflecting our inner life outwardly.

Is Not My Private Life, and Therefore My Home, My Own?
No. We were bought with a price (1 Cor 7.23)! Christ sets us free to have, as Michael Green puts it, 'A liberty to do as we ought rather than a licence to do what we want.'[37] It is demanding, yes, but it is an exhortation (1 Peter 3.21f). 'Our faith is always personal, but never private,' as Jim Wallis reminds us.[38]

Of course, some people may already have this discipline as part of their lives, or at least feel it is under control, despite the ever-increasing bombardment we all experience of goods and service providers. Bauman notes, however, that all human beings are, and always were, consumers.[39] This reality certainly preceded industrialization and modernity, let alone postmodernity. However, its pace now is such that the consumerist syndrome often sweeps Christians along without them adequately assessing their response to it.

Letting Go

One reason for not engaging in this process, often until long after it has become necessary, is that this process of decluttering is painful. Decluttering cannot be done dispassionately — far from it. This procedure is not a wholesale discarding of items without thought. Many things have memories of our past attached to them. Few people will discard a piece of furniture bequeathed by a favourite aunt, or a particular letter from a parent who has died, or maybe even that old school tie, or significant school report, or special holiday snaps. Even those who declutter for television programmes allow for retention of such items. In fact this is inherent in the decluttering process — we are left with what is important, not jumbled up with things we have kept for a whole raft of reasons.

But given this, decluttering is unlikely to be entirely pain-free. We all feel bereaved to some extent through loss. That bereavement, though, is a natural and, most importantly, a God-given process that needs to affect us if we are to travel on, released, into the future. In the process of letting go, we must face, assess, re-member (in the sense of giving reality again to what has meant so much to us), and lay to rest our attachments that are being let go.[40] Indeed, if we want to grow spiritually, decluttering will never be a clinical or emotionally detached process. We will always be letting go of some part of our old self to which we frequently cling so tightly.

Consumer goods all end up on some kind of rubbish tip, and they are symbols that mirror our shamefully wasteful society of excess. In the Western World, it should be to our embarrassment that most of our rubbish dumps would be Aladdin's caves of plenty to people in the Third World. Yet St Paul recognizes that plenty and want are both states from which to recognize the grace of God at work (Phil 4.12), for Christians have more lasting spiritual riches than the world provides (Phil 1.9f). We have the resurrection hope that began on the first Easter Day, and it is prefigured in the risen Christ. God renews us for a purpose, and a final eternal home awaits.

This is a real divine hope in the face of a secular world of discarded people, possessions and hopes. It enables us to see the true values of the world. Christians are called by the Lord to do what they can to witness the hope that is in them. Therefore decluttering should not be a one-off witness to the world, just as it is not a one-off process. It is a continuing response to a consumerist and acquisitive secular society that lives with situation ethics as norms, and derives its bases and morality from the market place.

The challenge is to witness effectively and communicate the gospel to a questioning society.[41] Over the centuries a didactic approach has predominated. We have worried about what people hear rather than what they see. Today, this needs to change in order that people may understand the gospel. It is not then a heresy to say that we embody, or should embody, the gospel. Most people do not read the Bible any more; but they do look at what Christians do and say. We must look like the values we say are different to a consumerist society that is mostly based on acquisitiveness. The Church of England report, *Towards the Conversion of England,* published in 1945, stated, 'Christians must take their part in re-creating a sound social and cultural life, and thereby healing the modern divided consciousness in which head and heart have become divorced and man's conscious purposes are no longer in harmony with the forces which give direction and tone to their emotional life.'[42]

If we take these words seriously, then a Christian's commitment must be not only towards right behaviour, ethical work practices, and a healthy family life, but also towards fashioning surroundings that reflect these concerns. We live in a society today where the 'Medium is *still* the Message' as Marshall McLuhan wrote in 1964.[43] We proclaim new life from our pulpits but the medium (that is, living in pretty much the same way as non-Christians do) is the message that is received by society. Christians do not influence the lifestyles of many in this country, for the common view of the church remains of a group that is conventional, oppressive to minorities, and ecologically indifferent. This message must change and be replaced by one that reflects our true beliefs.

The early church had a colossal task as it went out from Jerusalem into a world where there were few points of contact. They permeated polytheistic cultures, yet grew through the distinctive witness of ordinary believers testifying to a liberating God. They had nothing the world valued, but had found what really mattered (2 Cor 6.4–10). They were prepared to give an account of the hope they held (1 Peter 3.15), whether they suffered for their faith or not. We need to do the same. If others look and see something of the fountain of living water (Jer 2.13, John 7.38), then they will see a glimpse of God.

6

Decluttering is an opportunity we need to grasp.

Archbishop William Temple once wrote, 'The worst things that happen do not happen because a few people are monstrously wicked, but because most people are like us. When we grasp this, we begin to realize that our need is not merely for moving quietly on in the way we are going; our need is for radical change, to find a power that is going to turn us into something else.'[44]

We have seen that decluttering is a radical re-evaluation of the worth of possessions. Divesting ourselves of them is likely to be a painful process and one that must be done with care and sensitivity, both to self and family. It is a spiritual discipline when applied in a prayerful manner, seeking the guidance of the Holy Spirit. It is never a one-off event but an ongoing call to living with less physically, in order that we may find more spiritually. In the past the monastic tradition separated followers from ordinary life, but increasingly their witness of less needs to become part of mainstream Christian living.

It is suggested that decluttering our homes and living with less is a process that can have a double effect. It can provide more peaceful surroundings and enable our homes to be spaces where we might have a deeper sense of God's presence. Christians can then utilize such spaces to practise inward spiritual disciplines and reinforce the behavioural aspects of our lives that our faith requires of us. But also our homes will become places where those around us may see something of our God. Such witnessing is non-verbal and visual, but is more powerful than a preacher in our world today.

Such witnessing is non-verbal and visual, but is more powerful than a preacher in our world today

Christians can choose to mould their lives or be moulded by society around. Society today stresses individuality which fosters in its turn a loneliness, a distrust of neighbour, a suspicion of the motives of others and consequently little hope or meaning in life. In turn, there is a longing for spiritual reality in the face of confusion and *anomie*.

We require wisdom in understanding and assessing the pressures with which culture can overwhelm us, and have effective strategies to combat it. With decluttering woven into the fabric of our lives, we have a tool to do that, not only in terms of possessions, but also in terms of reinforcing our Christian pilgrimage of being transformed by the renewing of our minds (Rom 12.2). It means having a process whereby we can gauge the value of ideas, thoughts and goods in the world around us in the light of the Good News of Jesus Christ and its eternal dimension. At best, we can create far richer spaces than those provided by worldly experiences that are never, by definition, lastingly satisfying.

In a world where people seek peace from the cacophony of pressurized living, Christ's followers need to be attractive —an aroma of the gospel

In a world where people seek peace from the cacophony of pressurized living, Christ's followers need to be attractive—an aroma of the gospel. It is a witness in our lives that we are commanded to make, and in decluttering we have the possibility of doing so.

So, what might you get rid of that comes instantly to mind? What could you begin to give to others? What might you stop buying that fuels an addiction to things you know will not last? Just how much could you declutter your home and then your life, so that this world no longer governs your heart? Do not delay. Put this Grove booklet down and start the process *now*.

Happy decluttering!

Notes

1   www.statistics.gov.uk

2   Polly Toynbee, 'Narnia represents everything that is most hateful about religion,' *The Guardian*, 5 December 2005.

3   Survey quoted on www.religioustolerance.org/rel_impo.htm

4   Geoff Pearson, *Towards the Conversion of England* (Grove Evangelism booklet Ev 71); Steve Hollinghurst, *New Age, Paganism and Christian Mission* (Grove Evangelism booklet Ev 64).

5   Tim Lomax and Michael Moynagh, *Liquid Worship* (Grove Worship booklet W 181).

6   Russ Hughes, quoted in *The Church Times*, 12 September 2005.

7   *The Root of All Evil?* Channel 4, 9 and 16 January 2006. A critical response by an atheist is given by Neil Davenport (www.spiked-online.com).

8   Toynbee, *ibid*. She writes, 'Of all the elements of Christianity, the most repugnant is the notion of the Christ who took our sins upon himself and sacrificed his body in agony to save our souls. Did we ask him to?'

9   Jean-François Lyotard, *The Postmodern Condition: A Report of Knowledge*, trans: G Bennington and B Massumi (Manchester: Manchester Press, 1984) p xxiv.

10 See also Graham Cray, *Postmodern Culture and Youth Discipleship* (Grove Pastoral booklet P 76) p 22. The major postmodern issue for Cray is that of identity. His response is the construction of a distinctive Christian youth community.

11 Colin Horseman, *Good News for the Postmodern World* (Grove Evangelism booklet Ev 35) p 4.

12 Richard Rorty, *Contingency, Irony, and Solidarity* (Cambridge: CUP, 1989) p 84.

13 BBC News, 6 September 2001.

14 www.fairtrade.org.uk Suggestions for combating over-consumption are given by Lucy Siegle, 'How you can make a difference,' *The Observer*, 5 March 2006. Christians need to be informed on how they can conserve and share wisely and equitably the resources of a world that they know belongs to God, and for which they are accountable (Gen 1.28). See also Tom and Christine Sine's 'Living on Purpose' site www.msainfo.org/clop.asp and www.generous.org.uk for suggestions.

15 Julie Kelly, *Consumerism* (Grove Ethics booklet E 131) p 21.

16 Zygmunt Bauman, *Liquid Life* (Cambridge: Polity, 2005), and a series of similar titles.

17 *ibid*, p 2.

18 Hollinghurst, *op cit*, p 16.

19 Walter Brueggemann, *The Prophetic Imagination* (London: SCM, 1978), p 35. 1 Kings 6.12 has a telling clue; '*As to this house which you are building…*' The implication is that Solomon is not disobeying God so much as doing something God has not told him to do, but which is meant to impress countries and rulers around Israel. Nevertheless God's promise is given, dependent on the lifestyle of his people and the king. God dislikes being at people's beck and call (compare John 3.8).

20 F F Bruce, *The Epistle to the Hebrews* (Grand Rapids, Michigan, 1988) p 404. See also E Käsemann, trans R A Harrisville and I L Sandberg, *The Wandering People of God: An investigation of the Letter to the Hebrews* (Eugene, Oregon: Wipf and Stock, 2002).

21 Michael Green, *Acts for Today* (London: Hodder & Stoughton, 1993) p 37.

22 Colin Buchanan, *Ordination Rites in Common Worship* (Grove Worship booklet W 186) p 4.

23 Douglas Burton-Christie, *The Word in the Desert: Scripture and the Quest for Holiness in Early Christian Monasticism* (Oxford: OUP, 1993) p 47.

24 Wolfgang Simson, *Houses that Change the World* (Carlisle: Paternoster, 2001) p 80.

25 www.theage.com.au for 8 December 2005.

26 David Ford, *The Shape of Living* (London: Fount, 2004).

27 Robert Warren and Sue Mayfield, *Life Balance* (London: Church House Publishing, 2006).

28 Trans R S Pine-Coffin (Harmondsworth: Penguin, 1961). See also trans Henry Chadwick (Oxford: OUP, 1998).

29 For example: http://benwitherington.blogspot.com 'Christmas should be the day above all days where we don't stay home and open all those things we bought for ourselves INSTEAD of going to church. Christmas should be the day when we forget about ourselves for a few hours and go and honour the birthday of the great King, our Saviour.'

30 Quoted in *The Chicago Tribune*, 6 December 2005.

31 John Prizeman, *Houses of Britain* (London: Quiller, 2003) p 3. Prizeman suggests this is true for the exteriors of custom designed houses.

32 http://en.wikipedia.org/wiki/Minimalism#Minimalist_design

33 S Schleifer (ed), *Minimalist Interiors* (Köln: Evergreen, 2005) p 7.

34 For example, the Sanderson Hotel off Oxford Street in London transformed by minimalist Philippe Starck; see www.sandersonlondon.com for a visual webtour. The Starck design of shower head tap and attachment is a model of simplicity in form and function for shower and bath.

35 Ford, *ibid*, p 25.

36 Nick Helm, *Soul Spark* (Grove Spirituality booklet S 96) p 9.

37 Michael Green, *After Alpha* (Eastbourne: Kingsway, 1998) p 155.

38 Jim Wallis, *The Call to Conversion* (Oxford: Monarch, 2006).

39 Bauman, *op cit*, p 82.

40 This is explored more fully by Elizabeth Culling, *Spirituality and Remembering* (Grove Spirituality booklet S 56).

41 Pearson, *op cit*, p 14.

42 Credited to Archbishop William Temple. Quoted by Geoff Pearson, *op cit*, p 20.

43 His quote was 'The Medium is the Message.' Marshall McLuhan, *Understanding Media: The Extensions of Man* (New York: McGraw Hill, 1964). See also Mark Federman's essay on McLuhan's approach at http://individual.utoronto.ca/markfederman/article_mediumisthemessage.htm

44 William Temple, *William Temple's Teaching* (London: Macmillan, 1944) p 62.